DETECTIVE ACADEMY™

Forensic Analysis

by **Paul Mauro**
with **H. Keith Melton**
consultant

Scholastic Inc.
New York • Toronto • London • Auckland • Sydney
Mexico City • New Delhi • Hong Kong • Buenos Aires

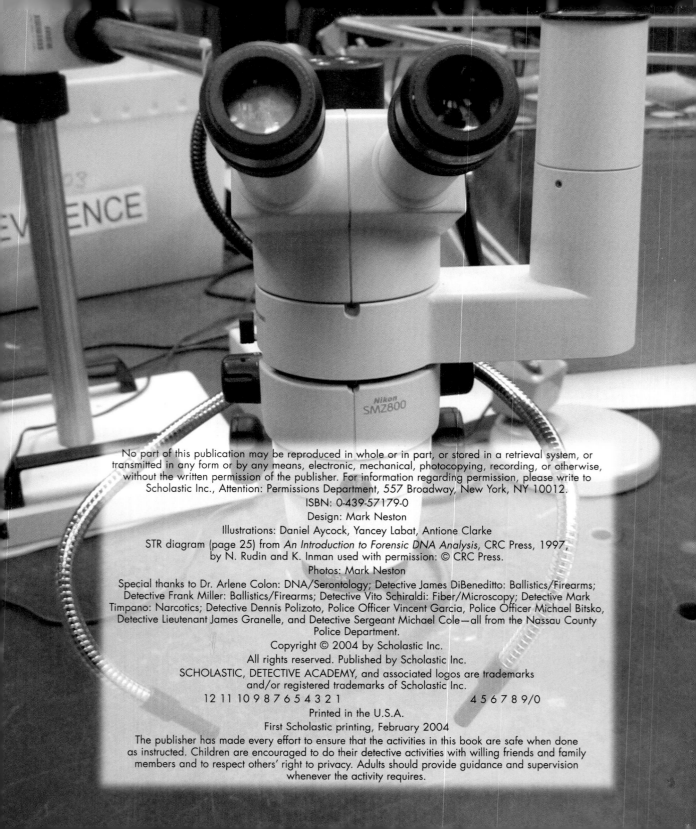

ISBN: 0-439-57179-0

Design: Mark Neston

Illustrations: Daniel Aycock, Yancey Labat, Antione Clarke

STR diagram (page 25) from *An Introduction to Forensic DNA Analysis*, CRC Press, 1997, by N. Rudin and K. Inman used with permission: © CRC Press.

Photos: Mark Neston

Special thanks to Dr. Arlene Colon: DNA/Serontology; Detective James DiBeneditto: Ballistics/Firearms; Detective Frank Miller: Ballistics/Firearms; Detective Vito Schiraldi: Fiber/Microscopy; Detective Mark Timpano: Narcotics; Detective Dennis Polizoto, Police Officer Vincent Garcia, Police Officer Michael Bitsko, Detective Lieutenant James Granelle, and Detective Sergeant Michael Cole—all from the Nassau County Police Department.

The publisher has made every effort to ensure that the activities in this book are safe when done as instructed. Children are encouraged to do their detective activities with willing friends and family members and to respect others' right to privacy. Adults should provide guidance and supervision whenever the activity requires.

Case Log

 When you see this symbol throughout the book, you'll know to use your **detective equipment** in the activity.

 When you see this symbol throughout the book, you'll know there's a related activity to be found on the Detective Academy **website**.

Magic? No—Forensic Science!

Hey, rookie—did you know that a single strand of your hair is enough to identify you from every other person on Earth?

Or that just one tiny thread from your shirt—or the ink in the pen you write with at school every day—could be almost enough to send you to prison if you were a criminal suspect?

How? *Forensic science*, that's how!

As you'll remember from your *Basic Training Manual*, a detective investigating a case is like a movie director. She's in charge, and it's her job to see that all the parts of the case are handled correctly—and that includes making sure that all the **crime scene** evidence is collected.

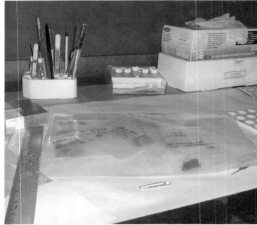

A forensic scientist's work station can include tweezers, rulers, sharp cutting instruments, and lots of plastic gloves.

But evidence collected by **crime scene investigators** isn't useful on its own. After all, even a fingerprint discovered at a scene is only useful if it can be matched to a suspect. And the same is true of physical evidence. Hairs, clothing fibers, handwriting, and ink samples...all these types of evidence have to be scientifically analyzed so that a detective can see who they point to.

And who analyzes that evidence? That's right, **forensic scientists**! They're the members of the police department who can examine something as simple as a strand of hair and, by using scientific tests conducted in a **forensic laboratory**, *prove* that it came from a particular suspect. They're like the magicians of the detective bureau. But it's not magic. It's science!

This heating lamp dries a narcotics sample that a forensic scientist is about to study.

FORENSIC LABS— THE CLUE FACTORIES!

Forensic scientists working in the lab will take the raw evidence found at crime scenes and spin it into investigative gold. By examining a single hair under a **microscope**, for instance, a scientist can tell you whether the person had straight or curly hair and what the person's true hair color was (even if the hair was dyed!). But they can do more. As you'll learn all about in this book, by using the super-powerful

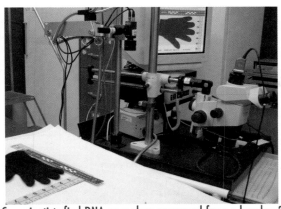

Can scientists find DNA on a glove recovered from a burglary? With their high-tech equipment, they just might!

investigative tool known as **DNA** analysis, a forensic scientist can sometimes match that hair to a suspect so perfectly that the odds are a *billion-to-one* that the hair could have come from anyone else! And *that's* the kind of evidence a detective loves to have.

In general, rookie, investigators send raw, sometimes confusing evidence to the forensic lab, and get back nice, clean clues. It's an amazing transformation, and it's all done with basic scientific techniques. Techniques *you* are about to learn!

And if science is your least favorite subject, don't worry! These methods are powerful, but simple. That's why science is probably every **perp's** least favorite subject. Forensic science has put thousands of them behind bars!

Detective Equipment

A big part of forensic investigation is using the proper equipment, rookie. That's why this month's detective gadget is a powerful microscope.

Microscope. This instrument, also known as a field or portable microscope, can magnify tiny evidence up to fifty times larger than its actual size—allowing you to conduct your own in-depth **forensic investigations**!

Four evidence slides. "Sandwich" two of your evidence items for examination with these slides. (Be sure to check out "How to Use Your Microscope" on page 9 for instruction on handling this equipment properly.)

Detective Academy Website

Want to learn more about forensic science? Or how about conducting a forensic investigation of your own? Log on to the Detective Academy website at: **www.scholastic.com/detective**.

Remember, you'll need your special password to access this month's feature. This month's password is: **inthelab**.

PASSWORD: INTHELAB

INSIDE A FORENSIC LAB

A **forensic lab** is set up to examine all sorts of different evidence. Check out the lab here to see the most common types of evidence **forensic scientists** analyze while looking for clues.

HAIR AND FIBER EVIDENCE

Forensic scientists use high-powered **microscopes** to examine hairs and cloth fibers found at a **crime scene** to see if this tiny evidence provides information about the **perp**.

DNA WORK STATION

Scientists place clothing or other items recovered from a crime scene on the blue-trimmed sheet on this work station. They then extract blood or other fluids that might contain **DNA** from the clothing and store it in vials.

SUBSTANCE COMPARISON AND IDENTIFICATION

Scientists test substances to identify what they are, or to attempt to match them to a possible perpetrator. Blood and DNA can be matched to a suspect. Narcotics, paint, and accelerants (like lighter fluid or gasoline) used in **arson** crimes can be analyzed by forensic scientists to see what clues they hold.

BALLISTICS

Forensic scientists test bullets recovered at a crime scene to see if they match to a particular gun, or if they are similar to bullets used in other crimes. These specialists also test recovered **firearms** to see if they were used in a crime.

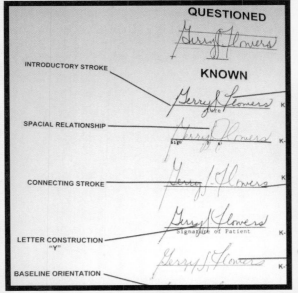

QUESTIONED

KNOWN

INTRODUCTORY STROKE

SPACIAL RELATIONSHIP

CONNECTING STROKE

LETTER CONSTRUCTION "Y"

BASELINE ORIENTATION

QUESTIONED DOCUMENTS

Forensic scientists examine all sorts of notes and writing to check for authenticity, and to see if handwriting samples can provide clues as to who the author was. Here, a signature made many times by the same person is being compared to check for similarities—or any suspicious differences!

DETECTIVE JARGON

When you see words in **boldface** throughout the book, check here to see what they mean. They'll have you talking like a pro in no time!

Arson: A crime in which a person sets fire to something on purpose.

Ballistics: The study of firearms and bullets.

To Collar: To arrest a criminal suspect.

Crime Scene: The area where a crime was committed.

Crime Scene Investigators (CSI): These are the police personnel or technicians who process evidence at a crime scene.

To Develop a Suspect: When a detective starts to gather evidence during an investigation that a particular person is guilty of the crime.

DNA: These letters stand for DeoxyriboNucleic Acid. Each person's DNA is completely unique and can be used to identify them.

Fiber Evidence: Evidence that involves threads from clothing, carpets, or furniture.

Firearms: Guns.

Forensic Analysis: To examine evidence using scientific methods.

Forensic Investigation: The use of scientific examination to solve crimes.

Forensic Lab: A laboratory that is dedicated to analyzing crime scene evidence in an effort to see who is responsible for a crime.

Forensic Scientist: A specialist who uses science to study evidence.

Forensics: The scientific study of evidence.

Grooves: Shallow scrapes cut into the sides of bullets by the rifling inside a gun's barrel.

Handwriting Examination: To scientifically analyze a person's handwriting, paying close attention to the size of letters and the way they are formed.

Homicide: A crime in which a person is killed on purpose.

Liquid Chromatograph: High-tech forensic equipment that separates the various chemicals that make up a particular liquid, allowing scientists to determine the exact composition of that liquid.

Microscope or **Scope:** A device which uses glass lenses to make small objects appear much larger when examined.

Perpetrator or **Perp:** A person guilty of committing a crime.

Questioned Documents: Any sample of writing requiring forensic analysis.

Rifling: Thin grooves cut into the inside wall of a gun's barrel.

Test Group: A collection of samples of a particular type of evidence that a forensic scientist uses to compare to new evidence.

To Toss: When police search either a prisoner or an area.

Trace Evidence: Small or minute pieces of physical evidence such as hair strands or clothing fibers.

To Type (Blood): Using scientific analysis to determine which of the four human blood categories— A, B, AB, or O—a person's blood belongs to.

Wet-Mold: Formed by placing an object to be examined under a microscope between two slides, together with a drop of water. This helps make objects "pop" under the microscope and become more visible.

How to Use Your Microscope

The **microscope** you received with this book is a powerful piece of equipment, rookie, so you want to make sure you use and care for it correctly. By following these simple instructions, you'll keep your scope operating at maximum efficiency:

- Set the microscope down on a flat surface, low enough so that you're comfortable as you look into it. You don't want to have to stretch up or over to see into the microscope's *eyepiece*; that would make it difficult to keep your head and eye steady (and give you a real pain in the neck!).

- Place a plain white, unlined sheet of paper under the microscope. This will provide a clean background for any items you examine.

- Turn on the microscope's *examination light*.

- When placing a *slide* beneath the scope, move the slide—not the scope. Slowly shift the slide under the microscope lens, until the object you want to examine comes into view. Then, holding the microscope with your right hand, use your left to slowly turn the *focus dial*, until the object comes into sharp view.

- To really make items "pop," try turning off your room lights while analyzing items under the scope's examination light. (But be sure the scope's examination light is on. Otherwise, you'll be experimenting with how long you can stand the dark!)

- For maximum magnification, set your scope to 50X. If you're looking at a bigger object, you might only want to set it to 40X.

- The scope is very sensitive; so try not to bump it as you look into the lens. Hold the scope firmly with at least one hand to steady it and move your eye to the scope (not vice versa).

Cleaning your microscope: The best way to do this is to avoid getting it dirty in the first place! So don't touch the evidence slides anywhere but along their sides, and try not to touch the scope lens altogether. If you do have to clean something off of the lens, use a paper towel. Wet it slightly, and gently *dab* (don't rub!) the lens. Let it dry on its own. Treat the glass slides the same way. For stubborn dirt, you can use glass cleaner instead of water.

Making a "wet-mold": Evidence items are often better examined in a "wet-mold"—it makes their features clearer and easier to see. When you make a wet-mold, simply place the evidence item on one slide, then add a single drop of water on top of the item. Close the mold by adding another evidence slide on top. And there you have it...the world's worst-tasting sandwich!

$funny $Money
ha $ ha $ ha ha $ha
$ haha ha ha ha

Here's a quick activity to warm up with, rookie!

The United States Treasury recently added some new features to American dollar bills ($5, $10, $20, $50, $100). These new features were designed to make it more difficult for counterfeiters to duplicate U.S. bills. Counterfeiters are criminals who make fake—or "funny"—money and try to pass it off as real. For that reason, some of these added characteristics are almost hidden— but you can find them with your **microscope**. Examining them in detail is a good way to warm up your **forensic** eyes!

Here's a picture of the front of a twenty bill, with a former president, Andrew Jackson, on it. Think you can guess where some security features are?

Give this a try and see if you'd be able to tell "funny money" from the real deal!

What You Do

Part I. The Real Thing!

1. First, ask a senior detective to *borrow* a twenty-dollar bill. (But remember— emphasize *borrow*! And be sure to return it when you're done!)

Security strip on bill's front, left side.

2. Now hold the bill up to a bright light so that you're looking at the front of it (with Jackson's face staring at you!).

Watermark on bill's front, right side.

Do you see the "security strip" that runs vertically just inside the bill's left side? Now look on the bill's right side. Do you see the faint image of Andrew Jackson? (This is known as a "watermark.")

3. Lay the bill front side up, on a clean sheet of white paper. In good light, look at the "20" on the bill's lower right side. Make sure your head is directly over the number. Do you see how the 20 looks shiny and bronze colored? Now, gradually move your head to your left or right—still watching that number 20. Once you've

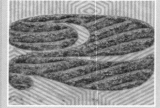

Looking at the numbers from the side.

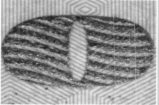

Looking straight down at the numbers.

moved your head a bit, do you see the bronze start to change to green? (These "color-shifting numbers" result from a complex printing process—and are very difficult for counterfeiters to duplicate!)

4. Now, place your microscope directly over that same number 20. Under the scope, do you see the raised, crystal-like structures that give the number its bronze tint?

5. Another unique aspect of American bills is the red and green fibers embedded in the paper. Can you find one of these? Once you do, take a pen, and make a similar "squiggle" next to one of the real ones. (You're only making a small mark, rookie, so it's okay to do this.) Now

SERIES 2004

examine both under the microscope. Do you see the difference between them?

These embedded threads are another feature of American money that makes it tough to counterfeit. Just drawing them doesn't cut it!

Part II. Passing the Buck

Okay, rookie—time for a little forensic work! There are two more anti-counterfeiting features on twenty-dollar bills. Can you find them? Here are a few hints:

1. Somewhere on the bill, "20" is repeated over and over—more than 20 times. Can you find them?

2. The words "United States of America" are written in an area near the big picture of Andrew Jackson. Can you find those words and the words that follow it? And one more point, rookie: An investigator's greatest asset is *patience*. So take your time. Does this bill get a "pass" or "fail"? You *have* to find that tiny writing to prove it's real—otherwise, it's fake! (Either way, check *Case Closed* to confirm your **forensic analysis!**)

What's the Real Deal?

Did you see in this activity, rookie, how your microscope can be used to pick up things your naked eyes cannot? The little details you were able to spot on that twenty-dollar bill are similar in many ways to the sort of forensic examination you'll be doing during the Case Files in this book. You'll be using your microscope to *carefully* and *patiently* examine various evidence items, to see what you can learn from them.

With recent advances in computer technology, counterfeiting of U.S. currency became a more common crime than it ever had been. And simple color photocopy machines were capable of turning out reasonably good copies of American bills—they weren't perfect, but they were close! That's why the bills have been redesigned. The hidden features you detected during your forensic analysis—like the color-shifting ink and the tiny printing—can't be duplicated by a photocopy machine. So now it's much, much tougher for those who wish to print fake money to get away with it. Most people don't even know these hidden features are there—and so, a casual counterfeiter is very likely to get caught. It's a serious crime—"funny money" isn't so funny after all!

Hair, There, 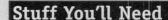 and Everywhere

Stuff You'll Need

- **Scissors**
- **Tape**
- **Some index cards**
- **Pen**
- **Evidence slides** DA
- **Eyedropper (optional)**
- **Microscope** DA
- **Notebook** DA
- **A fellow rookie**

You know, rookie, one of the best types of evidence out there is sitting right on top of your head: your *hair*. Because human beings generally lose about a hundred hairs a day, hair is one of the most common examples of **trace evidence** found at **crime scenes**. And because hair found at crime scenes can be used to match or disqualify to a suspect—by checking the hair's color, for instance—hair can be a valuable clue even *without* **forensic analysis**. But add **forensics** to the mix, and you've really got something!

Forensic analysis of a hair sample can be used to determine all sorts of things about a **perp**. Microscopic analysis can reveal if the perp's hair was dyed, for instance. Close observation of even short hairs can determine if the person had curly or straight hair. And hair can also be used as a source of **DNA**—the ultimate forensic tool.

So how *does* a **forensic scientist** actually go about matching hair discovered at a crime scene to a **suspect developed** in a case?

Keep reading!

What You Do

Part I. Pulling Hairs

1. Collect some hair! Go around to your family members, your fellow rookies, and other friends—even your dog, if you have one. See if you can get a couple of hairs from each of them. (See if they have any loose hairs on their shirt, or hairs left in a hairbrush, or see if they don't mind yanking a strand or two off their head to help advance science!) Try to keep all the hairs to about the same length. You can cut them to size using your scissors, if need be. As you collect the samples— two or three hairs from each person are enough—tape them to an index card. Label the index card with the name of the

person who gave you the hair sample. (Or, log on to **www.scholastic.com/detective** where you can print out customized Detective Academy labels.)

2. Now, it's time for some forensics! Take a hair from one of the samples and place it onto one of the evidence slides with a drop of water (use an eyedropper, if you have one). Then place another slide on top of it, making a "hair sandwich." Congratulations! You've just made a **wet-mold.** (This is the best way to examine dry evidence, rookie, as noted in *How to Use Your Microscope* on page 9.)

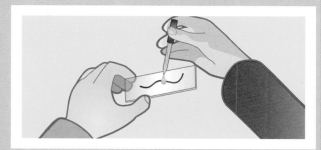

3. Study the wet-mold under the **microscope** and note down what you see. Ask yourself the following questions:

- What is the hair's color? Is it the same color the whole length of the hair? Or does it change color? Was it perhaps dyed?
- What is the thickness of the hair? Does it look fine (thin) or coarse (thick)?
- Does it look curly or straight?
- What is its condition? Is it frayed or damaged? Nice and smooth?

4. Now, go through each of your hair samples and make similar notes on each of them. Remember: Always examine the hairs using a wet-mold.

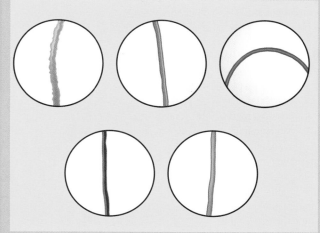

Part II. Gettin' a Bit Hairy

Now that you've got an idea of some of the characteristics hair can take on, rookie, test out your new knowledge!

1. Ask your rookie friend to make a wet-mold of a piece of hair from one of the samples you've collected—but make sure he doesn't tell you which one!

2. Study the hair under the microscope carefully.

3. Examine the notes you took in *Part I.* Can you tell which person (or animal!) this sample came from?

4. Now, *you* choose a sample and provide your notes to your rookie friend. Can he make the correct ID?

More From Detective Squad

For some more high-powered magnification matching, log on to www.scholastic.com/detective.

What's the Real Deal?

In this activity, rookie, you should have seen how people's hair can differ a great deal, and that a careful forensic analysis can lead you to the person it came from. By using careful observation, some of the unique qualities of each hair should have become clear to you. Once you have a record of those qualities, you'll know them when you see them again! And that's how a forensic scientist goes about matching hair samples.

To make matching hair samples a piece of cake, forensic scientists use special "side-by-side analysis" microscopes. They can look at a "known" hair sample at the same time as the "unknown" one.

Hair has been the undoing of many a perp. Criminals have unknowingly left pieces of their hair in gloves, in cars, in bank vaults...just about any place a crime could be committed! Especially in the event of a "heavy" crime—like a violent robbery or a **homicide**—**CSI** techs will scour every area of a crime scene looking for evidence of the perp. A hair can be a golden discovery. If a suspect can be developed, and that suspect's hair can be shown to have the same unique qualities of the sample found at the scene, that can be nearly as good as a confession. Hair, after all, doesn't get around on its own. Somebody has to bring it there!

CASE IN POINT — The Case of the Feline Felon

In 1994, Canadian police used hair found at a crime scene to solve a homicide. It was a highly unusual case. Why? Because the hair they found was matched to...a cat!

In the beginning of the investigation, detectives had little evidence—until they found a plastic bag near the crime scene. The bag contained a leather jacket with bloodstains that matched to the victim—and 27 white hairs. Forensic analysis revealed that the hairs were all from a cat!

The main suspect in the case was the victim's boyfriend, who detectives determined lived at home with his parents—along with an all-white cat. A specialist in cat biology was able to prove that the hairs on the leather jacket were a perfect match to the cat. So either the boyfriend was the perp...or that was one crazy cat!

With the help of the hair evidence, the boyfriend was convicted of the crime. For the police, it was a successful case. But for the perp, a pure *cat*-astrophe!

A Thread of Evidence

As you saw in *Case File #2: Hair, There, and Everywhere*, hair comes in all different varieties, and can be a great clue when trying to **develop a suspect** who was at the **crime scene**. But what if the **perp** didn't leave behind any hair? What if, after searching the crime scene, **CSI** comes up with **fiber evidence** instead?

Fiber evidence consists of thin strands of fabric that have accidentally been left behind by someone at the crime scene. And these threads can be excellent clues!

Unlike hair, people don't lose hundreds of fibers a day. (Unless you're still wearing that ratty old sweatshirt you've had since the second grade, which you should really throw away, rookie!) But clothing fibers *do* turn up at crime scenes (you'll learn how in the next case file). By examining fiber evidence, **forensic scientists** can tell a lot about what the perp was wearing at the time of the crime. This can be very important—not only can it tell detectives what the perp might dress like, but it also gives them something to match to if a suspect is developed. If the fiber is from an article of clothing the perp owns, that puts him at the crime scene...unless he's in the habit of lending out his clothes!

Stuff You'll Need

- **Scissors**
- **Tape**
- **Some index cards**
- **Pen**
- **Evidence slides** (DA)
- **Eyedropper** (optional)
- **Microscope** (DA)
- **Notebook** (DA)
- **A fellow rookie**

What You Do

Part I. Testy, Testy!

The best way to identify fibers easily, rookie, is to make a **test group**—a file of fiber samples you keep on hand to compare with any evidence fibers you find. This will let you know what sort of fiber evidence you have, and, therefore, what sort of clothing the fibers came from.

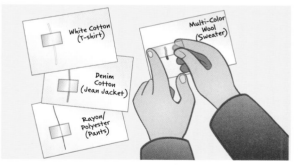

1. To make your own test group, start by gathering fiber samples from as many different types of clothing as you can. See if you can find any loose strands on the cloth. If you can't, carefully cut three or four threads off of each item (making sure you get a senior detective's permission—you don't want to ruin your dad's best suit!). Tape the fibers from each clothing article onto a separate index card.

2. On the index card, record the fabric type that's written on the tag, as well as the color of the item (blue cotton or green nylon, for example). Keep going until you've built up a test group that covers as many types of clothing as you can find.

3. Now, it's time to test your fibers. From each sample, make a **wet-mold** of one fiber, in the same way you did in *Case File #2: Hair, There, and Everywhere*. Examine each fiber carefully under your scope, and make notes on each type in your detective's notebook.

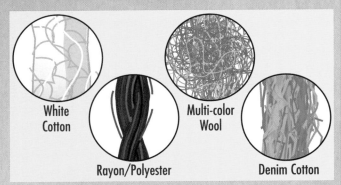

White Cotton

Rayon/Polyester

Multi-color Wool

Denim Cotton

4. Congrats! You've got a nice library of fabric samples. Your test group is established!

Part II. Matching Clothes

Now that your test group is set up, let's see how well it works!

1. Have your fellow rookie take a fiber sample from any of the strands you collected in *Part I* and present it to you—without telling you which it is!

2. Now, treat this fiber like true fiber evidence from a crime scene! Make a wet-mold, and examine the fiber under the microscope.

3. Using your notes, can you tell what type of fiber it is?

More From Detective Squad

There are fibers that need to be identified on-line at **www.scholastic.com/detective**. Log on!

What's the Real Deal?

Did you see how fibers can be used as effective evidence? Just one tiny strand of cloth can tell you something about what the perp was wearing at the time of the crime. But fiber evidence can do more than that. Once a suspect is developed, the fiber can be matched to an article of clothing the suspect owns, establishing that the suspect could have been at the crime scene.

In real life, rookie, fiber evidence is used much the same as hair evidence, in that it's valuable only if it can be matched to a suspect. At a serious crime scene, CSI techs will **toss** a room so carefully that even tiny fiber clues are discovered. Then, when a suspect is developed, forensic scientists can examine the fiber evidence so precisely that they can often prove that the fiber *had* to have come from a particular clothing item. By matching the color and the fabric exactly, the perp's shirt or sweater can be shown to have been at the scene of the crime. Confronted with that sort of evidence, many perps will save everyone a lot of time—and just confess!

Hanging By a Thread

As you've seen, rookie, matching **fiber evidence** can be very valuable when a detective is attempting to place a suspect at a particular **crime scene**. But sometimes, this type of evidence can be valuable even without it being matched. Sometimes, the key is not *who* left it there, but *how* it was left there!

When a **perp** leaves fiber evidence at a crime scene, it's almost always by accident. That means that the fibers either fell off the perp's clothing, or were *pulled* off. A strand of fiber that shows evidence of being pulled or cut could indicate that there had been some kind of struggle at the scene! The fiber can reveal to a detective something about what happened while that crime was being committed.

A **forensic scientist** examining fiber evidence will check for the condition of that fiber, looking for clues as to how it ended up being left behind. It takes careful analysis and a highly trained eye. But even a single thread can tell a detective a lot about what happened.

Don't believe it? Try this activity and find out!

What You Do

1. First, take your thread and, measuring by eye (you don't have to be *exact*), cut about 15 or 20 strands to about six inches in length each. (If you're using embroidery thread, separate out some individual strands from the thread.)

2. Once you've cut all the strands of thread, take a few—say four or five—and see if you can tear them in half. If you can't tear them, try ripping them using your teeth! (Do this carefully! You don't want to hurt a tooth!) Be careful not to mix up the torn strands with the rest of your thread. Once you've torn them in half, tape one of these threads to an index card, and label it, "Torn Fiber."

3. Now, take another four or five strands, and using the edge of a table or door,

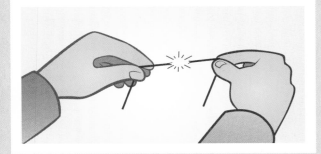

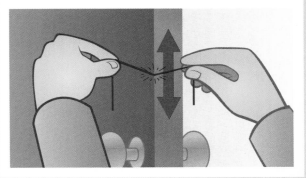

"saw" these threads in half. (Pull the threads tight as you do—they'll break soon enough!) Once you're done, take one of these strands, and tape it to another index card, labeling this one, "Sawed Fiber."

4. Take another four or five threads and, using your scissors, cut them neatly in half. Tape one of these to an index card, and label it, "Cut Fiber."

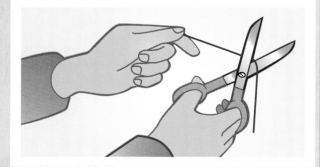

5. Now, before going any further, stop and examine your index cards. Do you see a difference between each of the three threads on the cards? What is it? (You can put each index card—with the thread still on it—under your **microscope** for a better look.)

6. Since you've only taped three fiber threads to index cards, there should be plenty of threads left over that you've broken in half. Mix them all together.

7. Once they're mixed, pull out one piece of thread. Make a **wet-mold** of it and examine the torn, sawed, or cut end closely under your microscope. Can you determine if it was torn, sawed, or cut? How do you know?

8. Keep going until you've discovered one thread of each type—a torn one, a sawed one, and a cut one. Compare them to the samples you've taped to the index cards to be sure you've found one of each!

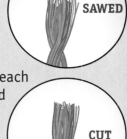

TORN

SAWED

CUT

What's the Real Deal?

Careful **forensic analysis** of a fiber can indicate just how that fiber was left at a crime scene. Remember: Fiber evidence can be very valuable—and no perp wants it lying around at a crime scene! That means that however it got there, it got there without the perp knowing. And that means it has secrets to tell—if you just know how to reveal them!

What an investigator is looking for is how "roughly" the fiber was removed from the clothing it was part of. If it can be shown that *many* fibers are present at a scene, and all were torn from an article of clothing, it's a good bet that some sort of struggle occurred at that scene. That's why fiber evidence of this sort is especially valuable at scenes where violent crimes might have occurred—like assaults, or even **homicides**. It's cases like these where the stakes are highest, and where a forensic scientist will look at every clue possible to find out exactly what happened. Sometimes, it will be a few tiny strands of thread that hold the answer to the crime!

Try Not to Faint!

Stuff You'll Need
- Washable red paint, or ketchup and water
- 3 pieces of cardboard or poster board
- Spoon
- Pen
- A fellow rookie

Rookie, one of the types of evidence that **forensic scientists** regularly have to deal with is blood. Like it or not, blood evidence is a part of the investigative process. It may be gruesome, but it can also be an important clue!

There are a number of ways that blood can be crucial to a **forensic investigation**. For one, blood can be **typed**; that is, a forensic scientist can test the blood to see if it is type O, type A, type B, or type AB—the four main blood types of human beings. Establishing the type of blood found at a **crime scene** can be important when trying to eliminate a suspect of a crime. This is a cheap and simple test that can eliminate suspects whose blood type doesn't match the sample from the crime scene. A more complex form of matching, which gives exact matches to a suspect but is also more time-consuming and expensive, is **DNA** matching (which you'll learn more about in the next case file).

Another way that blood can be important evidence is to examine the pattern of the blood splatter. Just like any other liquid, when blood hits something, it breaks up into tiny droplets. If someone is hurt during a crime, the *amount* of blood present—and the way it splatters— can tell investigators a great deal about what happened, as you'll see here. But try not to faint! Forensic science works best when the scientist is awake!

What You Do

Part I. A Plethora of Patterns!

1. First, you'll need some stand-in for blood! Talk to a senior detective about getting some red washable paint (that is, water-based paint). If you don't have paint, you can always mix ketchup with a little water (not too much or it becomes runny) to get a reasonably good version of fake blood.

2. Now, using your "blood" and your cardboard, let's examine some splatters! First, spread the cardboard on the ground (you'll want to do this activity outside because it's messy) and kneel over it. Dip the spoon into your "blood"—but

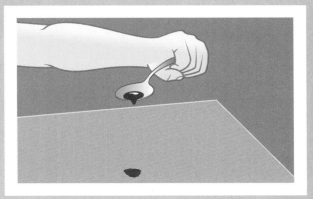

don't fill the spoon up. Just dip it! Then, holding the spoon over the cardboard, allow a single drop or two of the blood mixture to fall onto the cardboard. When you're done, take a close look at the results. How wide are the splatters?

How much did the drops break up? Take a pen and write "low-height drip" next to these blood splatters. Try this again to see if you always get the same (or a similar) result.

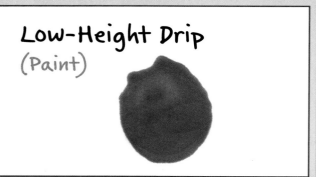

Low-Height Drip (Paint)

3. Now, on a separate piece of cardboard, try the same thing—except, this time, stand and hold the spoon. Now what do the blood drops look like after they hit the cardboard from a greater height? (Drip a few splatters to see if they all come out the same.) Label these splatters "full-height drip."

Full-Height Drip (Ketchup)

4. Now prop another piece of cardboard up against a wall. Using the spoon dipped in paint, flick some "blood" onto the cardboard. Examine the result. How does the pattern created by this blood differ from that of the paint you simply allowed to drip in Steps 2 and 3? Label this splatter "splash pattern."

Splash Pattern (Ketchup)

5. You've now got a permanent "catalogue" of some common blood splatter patterns! (And for some more fun, try saying "blood splatter patterns" five times fast!)

Part II. Test Pattern

Now that you have an idea of what some blood splatter patterns look like, see if you can identify them at a crime scene!

1. In an outdoor area—say, your backyard or in a local park—have your fellow rookie set up a fake crime scene. Using the same fake "blood" that you used in *Part I*, imagine that there was an attempted robbery, and that a struggle occurred. In two different spots of the

area, your friend should place some splatters using one of the three methods that you tested in *Part I*.

2. Now you—the forensic scientist—are going to inspect the scene! Examine the two areas of blood splatter. Can you tell how they were made? And if you can, what do you think that would mean if this were a real crime scene? What do you think "flicked" blood indicates? How about a couple of drops? (Check out *Case Closed* to find out.)

This blood drop found at a crime scene is measured to help determine the height it dropped from.

What's the Real Deal?

Did you notice how blood striking the ground—or an object—forms a definite, distinct pattern each time? By examining patterns in *Part II*, therefore, you should have been able to get an idea of how the blood splatters were formed. And once you know that, you have a good clue as to what happened to make each blood splatter look the way it does.

Investigators examine blood splatters for all sorts of reasons. In some cases, if there is blood splatter but no victim has been found, investigators might try to use the splatter to hypothesize about what happened to the victim. In other cases, the blood might be from the **perp**—and so, once again, investigators will try to figure out how the perp got hurt and by whom. (Was he cut while breaking a window? Did the dog bite him? There are all sorts of possibilities!) Either way, blood splatter evidence can be very important to a detective's case. That's why, to forensic scientists, blood splatters aren't just "a bloody mess." They're significant clues to be studied and analyzed!

21

DNA⚬⚬An Investigator's Best Friend

Rookie, if there's one area of **forensic science** that's changing detective work forever, it's the study of **DNA**. DNA—or DeoxyriboNucleic Acid—are super-tiny structures that exist inside every cell of your body. These structures contain all the information that makes you who you are—think of them as the "blueprints" of your whole body. As you grow, it's the DNA in your cells that tells your body what to become. Like a computer's memory, DNA stores all of your genetic information.

The reason this is so important, rookie, is that—as you probably know—no two people are alike. And since DNA exists in each of your cells, any evidence that comes directly from a **perp's** body—hair, blood, skin, even saliva—contains that perp's DNA. So, just from a little saliva found on, say, a cigarette butt left at a **crime scene**—DNA can provide a *billion to one match* to a suspect. But DNA is fragile and can be easily contaminated. It must be handled very delicately.

DNA testing is still evolving—it's becoming cheaper and it's being used more and more commonly in forensic science. A **forensic scientist** today *has* to have a complete understanding of how to analyze DNA to match it to a suspect. You should, too!

What You Do

Part I. In Search of Spaghetti

DNA is found inside every one of the billions of cells in your body—including your hair cells, skin cells, blood cells...everything!

Inside these cells are the various "cell structures," which you may have learned about in science class—things like the cell membrane and the

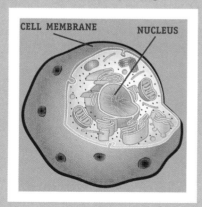

CELL MEMBRANE   NUCLEUS

nucleus. Inside the nucleus of the cell is where DNA is stored.

DNA itself has an odd shape, rookie, known as a "double helix." Taken together, all your DNA double helixes look sort of like a bunch of strands of spaghetti, all wound together into the cell's nucleus.

1. Now that you have an idea of

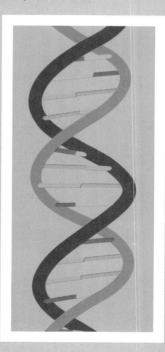

what DNA looks like—and where it's found—look at the following images. Imagine you're a forensic scientist about to start analyzing DNA from a blood sample found at a crime scene. Starting from what you can see with your naked eye—and then going all the way down to the microscopic DNA level—can you put the following three images in order, from largest to smallest?

When you're done, check *Case Closed* to see if you're right!

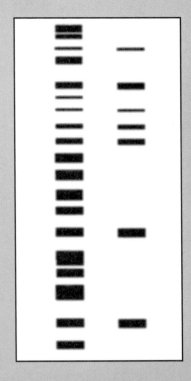

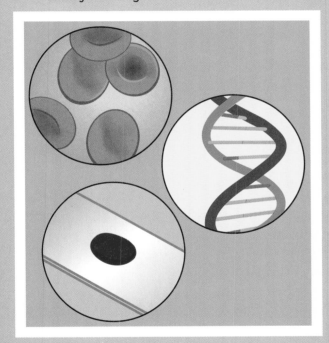

Part II. Breaking the Code

When forensic scientists analyze DNA, rookie, they need to put their reports into a format that people can recognize. (After all—this evidence could end up in front of a judge. And if that judge flunked biology, DNA clues could be meaningless!)

Scientists use a sort of "bar code" system to describe a person's DNA. After the DNA is analyzed and the scientists have determined the DNA's unique pattern, the bar code will look something like this:

Like the bar code you see on a cereal box, this one is used for identification. But here, these black bars describe the one-in-a-billion DNA code that this particular person has. And since no two people's DNA is the same, no two bar codes will be the same, either!

Imagine now, rookie, that the above DNA bar code sample is from blood found at a crime scene. Then, let's say you have a suspect in that case, but you want to be sure you've got the right person. Since you have a sample of the perp's DNA found at the crime scene, all you need to do is match it to your suspect's DNA!

1. What follows are three DNA bar codes from three different suspects. Can you match the correct suspect to the DNA above found at the crime scene? Check *Case Closed* to see if you have the right match!

A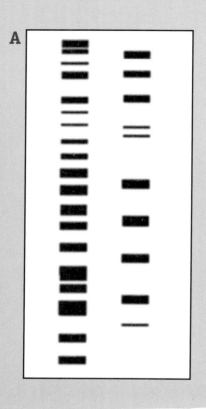

B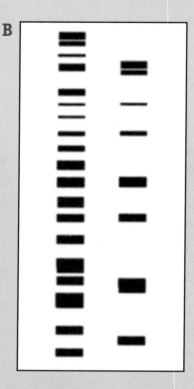

C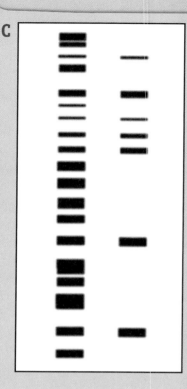

What's the Real Deal?

From this activity, rookie, you should have understood that DNA is the best way there is to identify someone or to exclude someone from a list of suspects. Because DNA exists in every cell of your body, all a perp has to do is leave just the slightest trace of himself at a crime scene, and a forensic scientist will have something to match to a suspect later on.

Detectives, **CSI** technicians, and forensic scientists rely on DNA evidence the most in their big cases. Because DNA analysis can be time-consuming and expensive, however, DNA testing isn't done in *every* case. But for serious crimes, DNA is relied on as a sure-fire way of showing that a particular suspect was at a crime scene. DNA is especially useful in these crimes because today's perps know a lot about detective work. (They watch TV, too!) So, many will wear disguises to avoid being recognized, and gloves to avoid leaving fingerprints. But there's no way to disguise DNA! If a suspect has left so much as a hair at the crime scene...he's nailed!

DET. HIGH-TECH!

Cleared By DNA

To say that DNA has caused a revolution in the forensics world is no exaggeration, rookie. The statistics are staggering. As of 2001, the state of Virginia alone was solving 10 to 15 crimes *a week* using DNA evidence! And over the last couple of years, DNA testing has become even more widely used. It's the gold standard of forensic evidence!

Because the odds of someone else's DNA matching your own is literally in the billion-to-one range, law enforcement now considers DNA evidence more convincing than any evidence that has been found before. For that reason, DNA is now being used to reexamine the cases of many people who have already been convicted and are serving time in jail. The result: Dozens of convicted felons nationwide have been granted freedom after DNA proved they weren't guilty. In some cases, those convicted have served more than 20 years in jail for a crime DNA proves they were innocent of!

Eventually, sending innocent people to jail will be a thing of the past. Why? Because DNA is now so readily available, it's being used to investigate just about every serious new case. When DNA material is available at the crime scene (blood or saliva samples, for example), it should be possible to all but eliminate the possibility of sending the wrong person to jail.

With a whole new version of DNA testing now available, known as "STR" (or Short Tandem Repeat), DNA analysis is even more accurate (and easier!) than before. Instead of using the standard "bar" system, STR gives a simple read-out on a computer screen, as shown here. Once again, it's science making things easier on forensic scientists, while making things tougher for criminals!

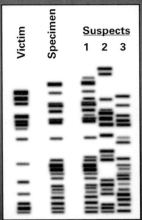

In these DNA bar codes, the DNA of three possible suspects is compared to the material found at the crime scene, as well as the victim's DNA.

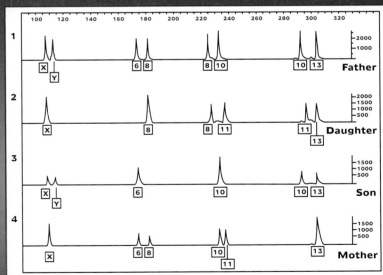

The new STR system of DNA testing provides simple computer screen results.

Going Ballistic!

Stuff You'll Need
- **Your sharp rookie mind**

As you've learned, rookie—anything a **perp** leaves behind while committing a crime can be used as a clue by expert investigators. A hair, a clothing fiber, a drop of blood containing **DNA**—all this evidence can tell a **forensic scientist** more than most perps would ever believe possible!

Another type of clue that forensic scientists can learn a lot from is known as **ballistic** evidence. Ballistics, in general, refers to anything involving **firearms**—guns and bullets. For forensic scientists, ballistics usually means analyzing bullets that a perp has fired—and so left behind—at a **crime scene**.

The reason scientists analyze these bullets is to see if they can match them to a particular gun. Say, for instance, a suspect robs a supermarket and, as he's fleeing the scene, gets into a shoot-out with the police. The suspect gets away, but the bullets he fired are recovered by **CSI** techs, who dig them out of the wall of a building across the street from the supermarket. Two weeks later, the same type of crime occurs in a nearby town. A good forensic scientist can now match the bullets from both of these crime scenes—and so, show that the same gun was used in each crime!

But the forensic scientist can do even more. Imagine that a perp is later arrested trying to sell stolen goods. At the time of his arrest, he has a handgun. As you saw on pages 6-7, scientists will now fire this gun into a water tank that stops the bullet without damaging it. They can then take this bullet and compare it to the bullets found at the scene of the two robberies. If it's a match, then they know that this gun was used in those two supermarket robberies. And that means that the perp selling the stolen goods is likely to be the perp who did the robberies!

For this reason, matching a bullet to the gun that fired it is a very important skill for forensic scientists. And since crimes involving firearms are obviously very serious—that's all the more reason to develop this ability!

What You Do

Take a look at this illustration, rookie—it shows a bullet before it was fired.

When a bullet is fired from a gun, the bullet portion leaves the gun at great speed. But the *shell*—the metal casing that surrounds the bullet—doesn't.

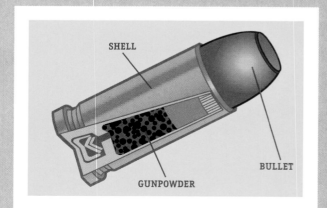

SHELL

BULLET

GUNPOWDER

As the bullet portion is shot out of the gun, it travels rapidly through the gun's barrel.

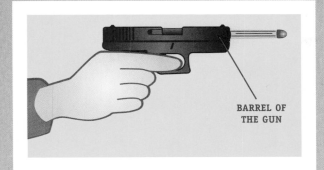

BARREL OF THE GUN

Depending on the type of gun, the shell either remains in the gun or gets ejected out of it.

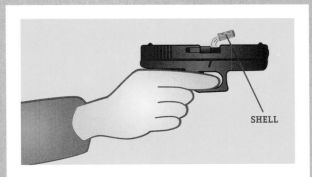

SHELL

On the inside of the barrel of the gun, there are a series of cuts in the metal. These are called **grooves**. The grooves make the bullet spin as it leaves the gun. This spinning makes the bullet travel more accurately to its target.

But these grooves also leave very distinct marks on the bullet. The grooves inside the gun that leave the marks on the bullet—called **rifling**—are how forensic scientists are able to match bullets to a particular gun. If the rifling marks on the bullet match the grooves inside the gun's barrel, the bullet must have come from that gun!

A gun with four grooves would leave a pattern like this on a fired bullet (with two grooves on one side, as shown, and two on the other side—making four grooves total):

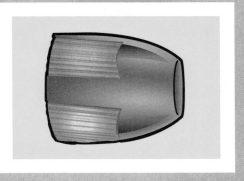

With six grooves, the marks would look like this (with three grooves on one side, as shown, and three on the other—making six grooves total):

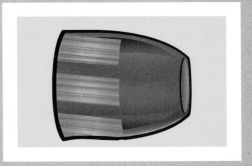

1. Imagine you're looking directly into the barrel of this gun, rookie. Note how many grooves there are.

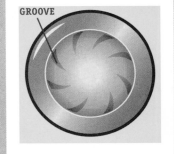

GROOVE

2. Now, imagine you're a forensic scientist attempting to match the bullets pictured on page 28 to this gun.

Try to make a match, then check *Case Closed* to see if you're right.

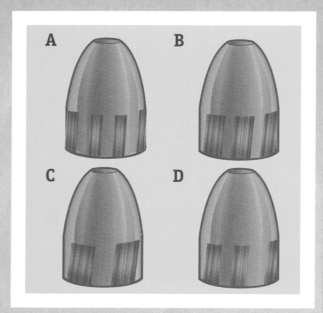

3. Now imagine you find these four bullets at *another* crime scene. Notice the shape of these bullets. That's often how they look after they hit their target. Can you tell which one appears to match the first bullet you found?

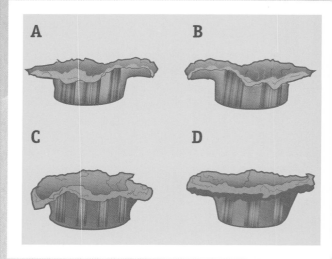

What's the Real Deal?

Did you see in this activity, rookie, how the rifling on a bullet can be used to show that it came from a particular gun? By matching the rifling marks that are left on the sides of a fired bullet, forensic scientists can prove that a certain gun fired the bullet. They can also show that similar bullets found at a different crime scene must also have come from the same gun. This puts the same gun at both crime scenes—and if that gun is in a suspect's possession, that's very powerful evidence that the suspect is the perp!

Investigators rely heavily on ballistic evidence. Sometimes, in fact, ballistic techs will go even further. Not only will they match the bullet from a particular gun, they can often show shells found at a crime scene are from a particular gun. When a shell is ejected from a gun, it receives marks unique to that gun, like bullets do. And, so, in the same way that fired bullets can be matched to a gun, the bullet's shells can, too. It's just another example of how forensic scientists can tell more from simple evidence than any perp would believe. And a good thing, too, because that's how perps get themselves caught!

DET. HIGH-TECH!

Ballistic Equipment

As you've probably figured out by now, rookie, technology is a key part of doing successful forensic work. As technology marches on and as new advances are made, new equipment becomes available that makes a forensic scientist's job easier.

Ballistics investigations benefit a great deal from high-tech equipment. One of the devices that is especially helpful for a ballistics investigation is known as a comparison microscope. Unlike the microscope you received with this book, a comparison microscope is solely designed for an investigator to compare two different items simultaneously. The two items appear in two separate "frames" under the scope, but side by side, so a forensic scientist can see if they match or not. This is especially helpful when trying to determine if two different bullets came from the same gun. Do the grooves on the bullets' sides line up? If they do—it's a match!

Bullets are studied under a high-powered comparison microscope, similar to the one you saw on page 14.

But what happens when an investigator has only one bullet to work with—or even just the bullet's shell? In that case, a forensic scientist can use a sophisticated computer system known as IBIS—the Integrated Ballistic Identification System. The IBIS system is a national computer database that stores the rifling marks found on bullets and shells discovered at crimes scenes. If detectives find either a bullet or a shell at a crime scene, they can input it into the IBIS to look for a match to the gun that could have fired it. It's very similar to doing a computer search for a fingerprint match. And just like fingerprints, if a match *is* discovered, investigators are much closer to making a **collar**!

In these two bullets, fired in the forensics lab to test them, you can see the grooves made by the gun they were fired from.

Know Your Writes

Stuff You'll Need
- 2 or 3 rookie friends
- A few ballpoint pens
- Some loose-leaf paper
- A ruler
- Notebook

Believe it or not, rookie, your handwriting is almost as unique as your fingerprints. Even though we're all taught to write more or less the same way, everybody adds their own little quirks and personality to the individual letters. Your handwriting is a way of expressing yourself. And it also identifies you!

Because handwriting can be so unique to a particular person, a document written by someone can often be matched to that person (which is one reason why getting your friend to do your homework for you is a very bad idea!). In cases where the author of a particular piece of writing is in doubt, a **forensic scientist** is able to use special techniques of **handwriting examination** to determine who the true author is.

Forms of writing that are of unknown or debated origin are called **questioned documents**—and they occur more than you might think in detective work. From ransom letters to bank robbery notes to forged (or faked) checks and wills, questioned documents have been a part of **forensic investigation** work since writing began. So you had better be able to tell what's real and what's not, rookie!

What You Do
Part I. Connect the Dots

1. First, gather your fellow rookies together and have each of them, using a plain blue ballpoint pen, write this sentence on the first line of a piece of loose-leaf paper: "The quick brown fox jumped over the lazy dogs." Make sure they write in script!

And make sure you don't watch them! When they're done, have them write their initials on the back of the paper.

2. To start your examination, first just look at the writing samples and compare them. What differences do you notice between them? Does one friend write with big, looping letters, while another uses a tighter, "chicken scratch" approach? How do the *size* of the letters compare? Pay special attention to the letters that begin and end words. Does each of your friends write particular letters the same way every time? Or do they vary? (Make note of your answer. That's part of a person's handwriting "style"!)

3. Now, take a second sheet of loose-leaf, and place it directly on top of one sheet with the writing on it, so that the papers'

edges are even. Under a bright light, make a little dot at the top of every letter in the sentence written on the bottom sheet on the top piece of paper. Then, using your ruler, connect these dots. Do the same for all of your samples.

4. Compare the samples of "top-of-the-letter handwriting analysis." What do you notice about how each sample differs? Does the height of each of your friend's writing samples stay pretty much the same? (And here's a bonus question, rookie: What do you notice about this strange sentence that each of your friends wrote? There's something quite unique about it. Can you tell what it is? Check *Case Closed* for your answer!)

Part II. Anonymous? Not!

Now that you have some idea about how to analyze a piece of handwriting, see if you can use it to nail a **perp**!

1. First, tell your friends that you're going to leave the room and, while you're gone, one of them should write a new sentence on a piece of paper. (Tell them not to think about it too much—just make something up and write it as they normally would.) Then step outside for a moment.

2. When you return, study the note carefully. Compare it to the writing samples you have from *Part I*. Can you match this new note to one of the other writing samples? Turn over the sample from *Part I* to read the initials of the person who wrote it and identify your writer!

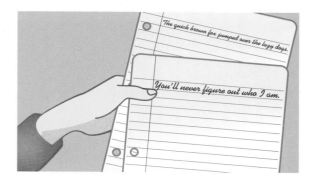

The quick brown fox jumped over the lazy dogs.

You'll never figure out who I am.

More From Detective Squad

For more handwriting analysis, log on to **www.scholastic.com/detective**.

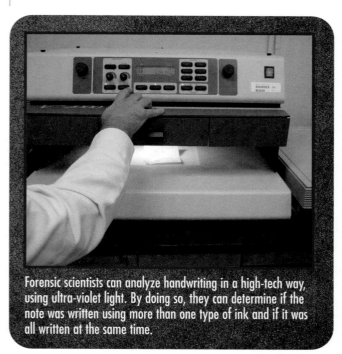

Forensic scientists can analyze handwriting in a high-tech way, using ultra-violet light. By doing so, they can determine if the note was written using more than one type of ink and if it was all written at the same time.

What's the Real Deal?

In this activity, rookie, you should have seen how **forensic analysis** of handwriting can be a very useful investigative skill. By comparing the characteristics of someone's writing—the size and "roundness" of certain letters, for instance, or the length and height of words—forensic scientists can identify two pieces of writing as coming from the same person.

The truth is, rookie, that faking someone else's handwriting is a lot harder than you might think (ever try faking your parent's signature?). Even though many people can do a reasonably good job of it, the vast majority of forgeries would never fool an expert (like a forensic scientist...or your teacher!). And this difficulty has been the undoing of many a perp! In hundreds of cases, detectives have taken a particular questioned document and matched it to another piece of writing that a suspect is *known* to have written—say, an old shopping list, or a letter he wrote to a friend. Once it's clear that the same person had to have written both samples, the **collar** is made. And the suspect isn't looking at a trip to the principal's office...he's looking at jail!

CASE IN POINT Identity Crisis!

One of the fastest-growing crimes today is identity theft—when one person steals the personal information of another, then uses that information to get credit cards, buy goods, and borrow money. But thanks to **forensics**, at least one identity thief will have to go back to being herself!

In March of 2003, California police raided the home of a 29-year-old woman against whom they'd developed evidence of identity theft. Inside, they found computer equipment, credit card information, and records of 27 separate stolen identities, right down to addresses, phone numbers, social security numbers, birthdays—even the victims' physical descriptions!

But the suspect wasn't home when the police raided her apartment. With nobody to question, detectives were stumped. They didn't have enough for an arrest, even though the woman had already used the information in almost $40,000 worth of crimes! (Even her apartment and phone were in someone else's name!)

That's when a forensic team examined the evidence, and a single clue turned the tables. Among all the documents, investigators discovered handwritten lists that contained the names of the victims. A forensic team was able to show that these lists were written in the same handwriting as other known writing by the suspect. In other words, the suspect had to have written these long lists of her victims. It was almost a confession: a list of people who'd all been tricked out of money, written by a woman who shouldn't have known any of them!

It was enough to charge the woman with over 20 counts of identity theft. When she returned to her apartment (unaware that police had been there when she was out), she was immediately arrested. This proves the wisdom of that age-old saying: Just be yourself!

CRIME in Fiction

Sherlock Holmes—the greatest fictional detective of them all—was no stranger to handwriting analysis.

In the *Memoirs of Sherlock Holmes*, Holmes is visiting a friend in the English countryside when two robberies take place. The first one, at the home of Mr. Acton, is very odd—only a few items of no value are stolen. During the second, at the home of the Cunninghams, a father and his son, a man is murdered—the Cunninghams' servant! A torn piece of a letter is found gripped in the dead man's hand. Can Holmes solve the case with this small bit of evidence?

"My dear sir," cried Holmes, "there cannot be the least doubt in the world that it has been written by two persons doing alternate words. When I draw your attention to the strong t's of 'at' and 'to,' and ask you to compare them with the weak ones of 'quarter' and 'twelve,' you will instantly recognize the fact. A very brief analysis of these four words would enable you to say with the utmost confidence that the 'learn' and the 'may' are written in the stronger hand, and the 'what' in the weaker."

at quarter to twelve learn what may

"Why on earth should two men write a letter in such a fashion?" [asked Mr. Acton.]

"Obviously the business was a bad one, and one of the men who distrusted the other was determined that, whatever was done, each should have an equal hand in it. Now, of the two men, it is clear that the one who wrote the 'at' and 'to' was the ringleader..." said Holmes.

"...We might deduce it from the mere character of the one hand as compared with the other. But we have more assured reasons than that for supposing it. If you examine this scrap with attention, you will come to the conclusion that the man with the stronger hand wrote all his words first, leaving the blanks for the other to fill up.

These blanks were not always sufficient, and you can see that the second man had a squeeze to fit his 'quarter' in between the 'at' and 'to,' showing that the latter were already written. The man who wrote all his words first is undoubtedly the man who planned the affair."

"Excellent!" cried Mr. Acton.

"But very superficial," said Holmes. "We come now, however, to a point which is of importance. You may not be aware that the deduction of a man's age from his writing is one which has been brought to considerable accuracy by experts. In normal cases, one can place a man in his true decade with tolerable confidence.... In this case, looking at the bold, strong hand of the one, and the rather broken-backed appearance of the other, which still retains its legibility although the t's have begun to lose their crossing, we can say that the one was a young man and the other was advanced in years...."

"Excellent!" cried Mr. Acton again.

"There is a further point, however, which is subtler and of greater interest. There is something in common between these hands. They belong to men who are blood-relatives. It may be most obvious to you in the...e's, but to me there are many small points which indicate the same thing. I have no doubt at all that a family mannerism can be traced in these two specimens of writing.... [These results] all tend to deepen my impression that the Cunninghams, father and son, had written this letter."

So why would the Cunninghams, together, write this letter? As it turns out, the Cunninghams were in a lawsuit with Mr. Acton. The first robbery was an attempt by them to steal an important document that would ruin Mr. Acton's case. The Cunninghams' servant had, by chance, seen them commit the robbery and was trying to blackmail them! Unfortunately for the servant, the note in his hand was nothing more than a trick to get him up to the Cunninghams' house, where he was killed. The Cunninghams then pretended that they had been robbed and that their servant had been killed by the robber. 33

An Ace in the Hole

Hey, rookie—imagine you're the detective working the following case. Two **perps** robbed a local gas station store. The perps were standing in front of the counter and the station clerk ducked down as shots rang out!

As part of your investigation, you need to figure out which perp made which bullet hole. Was there a third perp outside who fired his weapon? Did one perp shoot twice? With no suspects in custody, how will you figure this one out?

Forensics!

When a bullet penetrates a wall, it makes a very distinct hole. This hole will not only bear some impression of what the bullet looks like, it will also demonstrate the *angle* the bullet hit at. **CSI** processing a **crime scene** will take careful, detailed photos of a hole like this. And by examining the photos, and the angle the bullet struck at, a **forensic scientist** can demonstrate where the bullet must have been fired from.

Check out the case below, to see how it works.

What You Do

1. First, look at the picture below. It shows a bullet that was fired straight on at a wall. Notice how the bullet has made a straight hole?

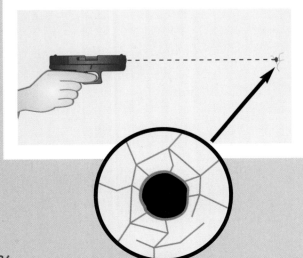

2. Now, check out this picture. This is of a bullet that was fired from *above* the hole, and at an angle. Do you see how the angle from which the bullet was fired is reflected in the hole the bullet made? In this case, the "tube" goes down and away from us because the bullet was fired from above and behind us!

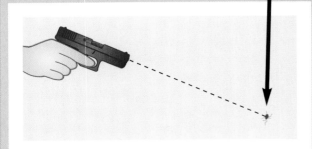

3. Now, take a look at the crime scene below. The clerk states that as he ducked, Perp A pointed a gun right at him. He also swears that he only heard one shot. Can you tell which perp made the bullet holes, based on the angle of entry for each one? When you're done, check *Case Closed*!

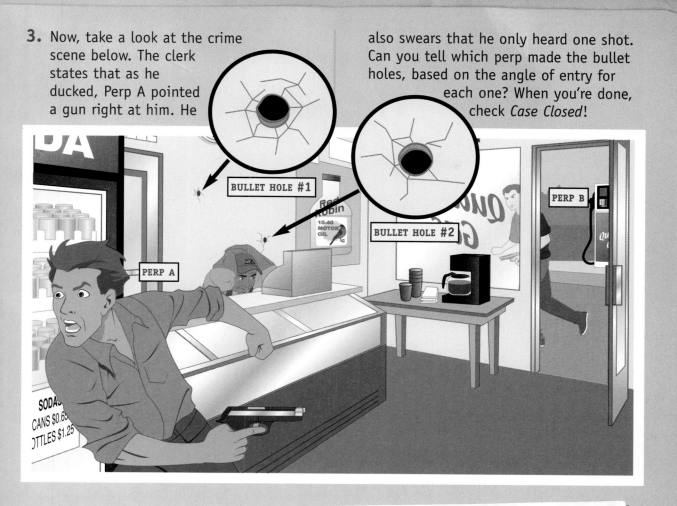

BULLET HOLE #1

BULLET HOLE #2

PERP B

PERP A

What's the Real Deal?

By following the angle back to its origin, a forensic scientist—like you!—can demonstrate where the perp must have been when he fired the shot. It's just a question of checking that angle of entry, then following it backwards.

In real life, forensic scientists use a number of tools to examine a bullet hole of this sort. A long metal rod that resembles the antennae from a portable radio is inserted into the bullet hole. By watching what angle the antennae sits at, scientists can determine what angle the bullet traveled into the wall at and where it was fired from. In some cases, if a bullet has hit *two* objects—say, it went through a window and then got lodged in a wall—techs will shine a thin, laser-like light through the window hole, so that the light beam lines up with the hole in the wall. Wherever the scientist must stand to make that light beam go through both holes, that's where the bullet was fired from!

Break It Down

Stuff You'll Need
- Scissors
- Some paper coffee filters (or try plain white paper)
- Ruler
- Some pens that are all the same color (like a permanent marker, felt-tipped pen, gel pen, or highlighter)
- A glass of water
- Some paper towels
- A rookie friend

One of the things that **forensic scientists** are often concerned with, rookie, is not only *matching* evidence, but *identifying* it. There are many times when **CSI** will process a substance at a crime scene—from an **arson**, for instance—and not even be sure what that substance *is*! Is it gasoline used to start the fire? Or is it rubbing alcohol someone spilled? Send it to **forensics**—let them figure it out!

In order to identify a mystery substance, forensic scientists usually have to get high-tech. They'll turn to the special machinery that **forensic labs** are stocked with to break a substance down into its basic parts (this allows it to be studied more easily). And if the substance is a liquid, chances are they'll use a nifty little device called a **liquid chromatograph** (pronounced kro-mat-o-graf).

Don't let the name scare you, rookie! A liquid chromatograph is simply a box-like device about the size of a microwave oven that separates a liquid into the various chemicals that went into making it. By heating the liquid and then dividing it up into parts, the chromatograph allows scientists to analyze each part separately. And that lets them know what they've got!

One substance that is sometimes given the chromatograph treatment is ink. If, for instance, a detective has a ransom note that he wants to prove was written with the ink from a particular pen, he's got to show that the inks match. By breaking down the two samples—the ink from the note and the ink from the pen—inside a chromatograph, the detective can show that the inks have the same ingredients.

Try this activity, to get an idea of how a chromatograph works.

What You Do

Part I. You Gotta Keep 'Em Separated!

1. First, cut the coffee filters up into strips about an inch wide and a few inches long.

2. Now, using one of the felt-tipped pens, draw a circle about the size of a nickel on one of the strips, toward one end of the strip.

3. Pour some water into a glass, and dip the tip of the paper strip with the ink mark on it into the water. Don't wet the ink, rookie—just dip the tip of the paper in, and hold it there. You'll notice that the water slowly creeps up the coffee filter strip toward the ink circle you made. (If your hand gets tired, fold the paper over the lip of the glass and let it sit for a while—the strip will stick to the side of the glass by itself.)

4. Once the water has covered pretty much the whole strip (it should only take a few minutes, unless you use plain white paper, which could take a few hours), put the strip on a piece of paper towel to dry.

5. Now, repeat the same process with a different pen. As you do, identify the wet strips of coffee filter by writing down which pen was used. Write the pen type right next to the ink spot, on the paper towel. Don't write on the wet filter strips!

Permanent Marker

Fountain Pen

Highlighter

6. Keep an eye on the paper strips as they dry. Do you see the pattern of colors forming on the strips as the original color breaks down? Congratulations! You've just separated the chemicals in that ink!

Part II. Busted!

Make sure you leave the paper strips from *Part I* in place on the paper towels, rookie, so that you know what their original ink colors were. Now, let's see if you can put this technique to work...to solve a case!

1. You're a forensic scientist who has to identify the ink on a ransom note. Have your fellow rookie write a fake ransom note on another strip of coffee filter. Tell him to use one of the pens you used in *Part I*—but make sure he doesn't tell you which one! Leave the room while he writes, so you don't see which pen he uses.

2. Once he's done, come back into the room and perform the water test on the ransom note, as you did in *Part I*. Compare the broken-down note with the strips you made. Can you figure out which pen was used to write the note?

Leave $50 in the mailbox or you'll never see fido again!!!

What's the Real Deal?

By breaking something down into its parts, a forensic scientist can study it, thereby identifying it and matching it. While the water method isn't as high-tech as a liquid chromatograph, it can sometimes work just as well! A forensic scientist can use this technique to show what chemicals were used to make up a certain liquid. And now that she knows exactly what that liquid was made of, she can attempt to match it to another sample liquid.

Forensic scientists rely on liquid chromatographs to break down all sorts of liquid evidence. Just about any liquid that is *inorganic*— that is, it does not come from an animal or human being—can be separated out inside of a chromatograph. Scientists use the machine to show the composition of paint found on a weapon, ink used on a forged document, chemicals used to start fires—all sorts of liquids used at **crime scenes**. So don't be scared off by the name. As a forensic scientist, a liquid chromatograph is one of the best friends you have!

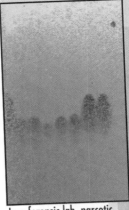

In a forensic lab, narcotic substances are tested using a chromatograph.

CASE IN POINT

Burned— By Forensic Science!

Back in 1990, a California man was so upset that his sports souvenir store burned down, he put up a $10,000 reward for information about how the fire had started. But once forensic science got involved, it was a sure thing that the reward would never be paid!

The fire not only completely destroyed the store, which was stocked full of expensive and rare sports memorabilia, but a nearby building as well. Yet even after losing everything, the owner opened a second store across the street from the first.

But since the fire had burned so intensely, suspicions were aroused. Using chemical analysis of materials found at the crime scene, forensic scientists were able to prove that the case was arson—that is, the fire had been set deliberately!

Armed with this information, detectives began to interview suspects. Eventually, the investigation led them to charge one suspect with paying to have the fire started. Who? Put it this way: The owner had been happy to offer a hefty reward because he knew he'd never have to pay it. He had paid to have his own store burned down!

Evidence taken from crime scenes where arson is suspected is sometimes stored in paint containers, like these, before forensic scientists examine them.

It seems the owner stood to receive $325,000 in insurance money from the fire. Money he would have gotten, too—if the forensics team hadn't stepped in and charged him with the crime!

Chipping Away

Stuff You'll Need

- A small amount of a few different color paints
- A small piece of wood
- Screwdriver
- White paper
- Pen
- Microscope (DA)
- Evidence slides (DA)
- Notebook (DA)

As you may have noticed by now, rookie, **forensic** science is all about *matching*. In many of the activities in this book, you've learned forensic techniques for identifying items that go together. Whether matching hair to a **perp's** head, fibers to his jacket, or bullets to his gun—you've been trying to show that these two items *had* to be attached at one point!

Forensic scientists take the same approach to another item, rookie—*paint*. Because dry paint can flake or chip—and then stick to something—it can be a very effective forensic tool when you're trying to place a perp at a particular **crime scene**.

One area this technique is particularly useful in is **forensic investigations** of auto accidents. Because all cars are painted, a vehicle collision will almost always leave a few specks of paint on whatever the car hit (and sometimes vice versa). So if, for instance, a person driving a black car bangs into a parked blue car, both cars will be a little black and blue!

Of course, there are other ways that paint can be useful as evidence. Say a burglar uses a screwdriver to pry open a window—there's a good chance there'll be some tiny paint flecks clinging to the screwdriver's head. Or, let's say that burglar then squeezes through the window—he could scrape a bit of paint off on his shirt or pants. Once forensic scientists match the paint on his pants or on the screwdriver with the paint around the window, it puts that perp at that **crime scene**. He's met his match!

Think *you* can tell which paint samples go together?

What You Do

Part I. Feeling Chipper

1. Start by collecting some paint samples. But wait—don't start scraping at your mom's car! See if you can get a few paint samples around the house *without* damaging anything. Try looking next to an old bicycle or lawnmower in your garage—or around the molding of a window that hasn't been painted in a long while. If you can't find any paint

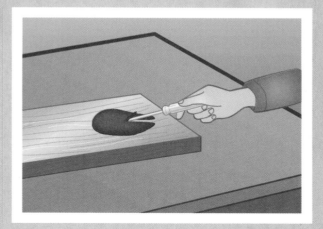

chip samples (they can be tiny), you'll have to make them! So with the permission of a senior detective, get some paint together. (You can even use nail polish if you like!) You'll need at least two or three different colors. Once you have them, put a few small blobs of paint on an old piece of wood, then wait for them to dry. Once they do, just chip them off using a screwdriver and you're in business!

2. Now, place one of your paint chips on a plain piece of white paper. Label the paper with the paint's color, then examine the paint chip under your **microscope**. Do the same for the other colors of paint you have samples of. Aside from the different colors, are there any other distinctions you see between them? Does one have more cracks in it? Is one smoother? Does one appear more "flaky"? Note your observations about the quality of each paint chip in your detective's notebook.

Part II. Pick a Color, Any Color!

1. Now that you know what paint chips look like under magnification, announce to your folks or some fellow rookies that you're going to dazzle them with some forensic magic! First, get together two different types of *the same color paint*. (You can use finger-paint and nail polish, or shoe polish and house paint...it really

doesn't matter. But make sure you use two different types and that they're the same color!)

2. Prepare a "chip sample" of both paints, just as you did in *Part I*. Study each, and make notes again—careful notes. Remember: You won't be able to tell them apart just by color this time. So be thorough, rookie—this one counts!

3. Now invite your friends or family into a room and tell them that, when you leave the room, they should put a little dab of one of the two paints on a piece of wood. Let them know that no matter which of the paints they choose, you'll be able to tell which one it was!

4. When you return, scrape off some of the dried paint they chose, and examine it under your microscope. Refer to your notes. Now tell them which paint they chose!

What's the Real Deal?

Did you see how examining and matching paint samples can be a highly effective forensic tool? We don't really think about it too often—lots of everyday stuff is painted. But when two things collide, they very often leave a little paint where they make contact. By matching paint chips—no matter how tiny—with the paint they came from, you can show that these two objects came in contact at some point.

Investigators will use this sort of analysis most commonly to solve hit-and-run vehicle crimes. If a person driving a car hits another car—or even strikes a building—that collision will almost always leave a paint sample on whatever object was struck. Because there are so many cars out there—and because it's so easy for someone driving a car to flee a crime scene—leaving-the-scene crimes are very common. So forensic investigators rely on matching paint chips at the collision scene with the paint on a suspect's car to prove that this is the car they're looking for.

CASE IN POINT

CONNECTICUT
GOT-U
CONSTITUTION STATE

In 2001, detectives in Connecticut conducted an in-depth investigation into a hit-and-run accident that seemed almost impossible to solve. But **forensic analysis** of some paint chips was just enough to lead investigators in the right direction.

After the accident, the only clues detectives had to go on was a piece of license plate showing just two partial numbers or letters of the full plate and some gray paint chips. Would these be enough for the investigators?

Yes! One of the detectives was able to identify a letter—C—and number—2—on the partial license plate. Then forensics provided a key discovery: The gray paint chips matched paint used on General Motors cars made from 1987 through 1992. The investigators set about looking for a gray car made in one of those years, with the letters "C-2" in a Connecticut license plate.

They got a match with the partial license plate! Detectives now had the name of the owner of the car. And when they tracked him down, they found that the paint chips from the crime scene matched the car's paint. Confronted with the evidence, the driver claimed he'd known he hit something, but wasn't sure what. The detectives didn't buy his story, and the case was closed by arrest.

FORENSIC SPECIALISTS

Rookie, as you probably know, there is more than one branch of science. So guess what? There is more than one branch of **forensics** as well! And there are **forensic investigators** that specialize in some of the more unusual evidence types. So keep reading—and meet the experts that use their unique abilities to help detectives get their **perp**!

FORENSIC PATHOLOGIST

Among all forensic investigators, there's one that has a particularly unique and difficult job. A forensic pathologist is an investigator with medical training who does tests and examinations on biological evidence—usually, a dead human body.

Forensic pathologists—who are sometimes called coroners or medical examiners—have the difficult task of determining the cause of death in cases of suspected **homicide**. In some instances, why the victim died isn't entirely clear. So in order to find out, a forensic pathologist will perform a procedure known as an autopsy. In an autopsy, the examiner will surgically examine the body to find out what caused the death, and decide whether it's a

homicide, or if the person died from an accident, suicide, or of natural causes.

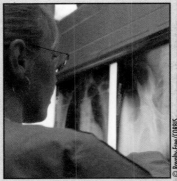

A forensic pathologist examining X-Rays.

Like other forensic investigators, forensic pathologists bring not only their unique skills to the job (in this case, their medical skills), but also their police training. By examining wounds and testing biological evidence, a forensic pathologist is a combination doctor-detective. And as you can imagine, they need one more thing: a strong stomach!

FORENSIC PSYCHOLOGIST

Forensic psychologists are highly trained and educated professionals who conduct investigations using *psychology*—the study of the human mind. Unlike regular psychologists who help troubled people cope with emotional or behavioral problems, forensic psychologists often spend their time examining **crime scenes**, and then offering suggestions as to what sort of person might have committed the crime.

One forensic psychologist who has worked on many cases is Katherine Ramsland.

"I've gone out on cases with **crime scene investigators** and been asked to give my impressions. Sometimes, you're trying to determine if a scene is a homicide or a suicide. A forensic psychologist helps interpret the scene. I'll do

interviews and look into the victim's background. By helping to interpret this person's state of mind, I can help the police fill in some of the gaps. And if it's a homicide, I'll give them an idea of what kind of a person would commit a crime like this.

Katherine Ramsland, Ph.D.

My day is spent working on case reports and reading new psychology information. But I'm always ready for that next phone call. That's the one thing that makes this work unusual. Every day, there is the possibility that I'm going to be called by an attorney, a police officer...somebody asking for information or assistance on a case that suddenly plunges me into a whole new demanding experience."

FORENSIC VIDEO ANALYST

As you've learned, rookie, a forensic investigation uses science to study evidence in a criminal case. But that evidence isn't limited to just hairs and fibers. It also can involve videotape! Banks, department stores, and even many schools and offices have video cameras that record everything that goes on. So if a crime occurs there—it's on tape!

Unfortunately, because of technical malfunctions or poor lighting, the video that investigators of a crime actually end up with is often less than perfect. In fact, because security personnel often simply re-use the same tape over and over (taping over what was previous recorded), the quality of the video can be very poor.

And that's where a forensic video analyst comes in. This expert uses computer programs and specialized equipment to "enhance" the video—that is, make it clearer, so that investigators can actually see what's on the tape.

Sergeant Conor McCourt of the New York City Police Department is a forensic video technician who has "cleaned up" dozens of poor-quality videos. "Sometimes, the images are dark or obscured. There's often some tape damage. We can 'clarify' it—slow it down, zoom in, adjust the brightness. We can also remove the static, and pull up images like a license plate, or a person or object that's there. It's not always just

Sergeant Conor McCourt

about cleaning up the image. It's about looking at the tape, not just as a technician, but as an investigator as well. Maybe you can't totally clarify the perp's face—but maybe that's not so important if you can show where he put his hands. Now we know where to look for fingerprints. Or maybe you can clarify a clothing item, to see if we can match it to a suspect later. See, you need police experience, as well as technical know-how. That's really what makes a good forensic video analyst."

An image of a car from a poor quality videotape.

The same car image "cleaned up."

The license plate of the same car has now become more visible.

On the Job: At Work with **FBI Special Agent** and **Forensic Scientist** **Gerald Richards**

Former agent Gerald Richards, now retired after 23 years in **forensic** work with the Federal Bureau of Investigation (FBI), started out as a forensic examiner of evidence photographs. He became the Chief of the Special Photographic Unit of the FBI.

Over the years, Agent Richards developed a number of forensic specialties, including **questioned documents** examination. He also developed a special eye for seeing the important details in evidence photos. For instance, he became an expert in matching clothing seen in photos to real-life clothing. "Once we had a video of a bank robber wearing a certain shirt, but his face wasn't visible. He later was arrested for committing another crime and a search of his house revealed a shirt similar to the one in the bank robbery video. We proved that this was the same shirt from the video of the robbery by carefully examining the shirt's pattern, right down to the stitching. You see, even shirts with a similar pattern are unique in the way they're sewn together. A **forensic analysis** can reveal that."

In another of Agent Richards' cases, a team of bank robbers accidentally tore a ten-dollar bill as they were taking it out of the cash drawer. Later, when they stopped to divide up the money, they realized the bill was torn, and that the other half was still in the bank. So rather than burn their half, or just get rid of it—they buried it! Later on, when one of them was caught for another crime, he informed on his partners. "He led us to the buried bill, and I was able to show that the two halves matched—and that the bank robber in custody was telling the truth about what happened."

Agent Richards' typical day would start with checking where his cases stood. "The first thing I would do is see if we had any emergencies—if we had any cases that had to be worked on right away for a trial. If we had a very serious case, we'd start with that. Otherwise, we'd start with the oldest case, so we could keep our caseload up-to-date."

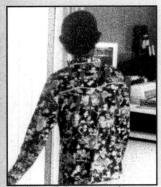

A photo of the perp at the crime scene—wearing the shirt in question.

The same shirt worn for examination after it was recovered at the perp's house. The red arrows point to the identical stitching on each shirt.

Case of the Armed Robbery

I. The Facts

A serious crime has occurred—an armed bank robbery!

A **perp** entered the First National Savings Bank and quietly slipped the teller a note demanding money. The teller gave it to him, but as the robber was leaving the bank, the teller notified the security guard. That led to an exchange of gunfire between the guard and the robber. The security guard wasn't hurt, but even though the perp was grazed by a bullet, he escaped.

II. The Evidence

After the first responders seal the area and **CSI** processes the scene, the following evidence is discovered:

1. A bullet fired by the perp, dug out of the wall of the bank.

2. The note that the robber handed the teller.

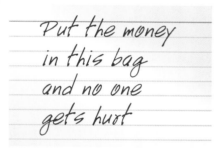

Put the money in this bag and no one gets hurt

3. Three fibers, which appear to match a tattered jacket that the teller says the perp was wearing.

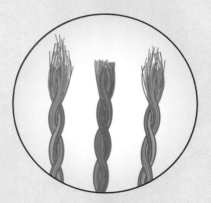

4. One hair, recovered near the teller's booth where the perp was standing.

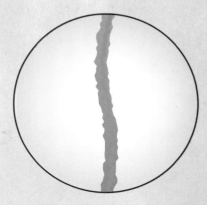

5. Some dried blood drops, from the perp's graze wound, found on a section of carpet near the bank's front door. **Forensics** later determines them to be type O blood.

III. The Suspects

Three suspects of the crime are **developed**, rookie. They are:

Richard Mantellino

Jack Leetch

Kieran O'Sullivan

Both Richard Mantellino and Jack Leetch admit to being in the bank that day (both claim they were just doing their banking). But Kieran O'Sullivan says he's never been in that bank in his life.

Armed with search warrants (legal authorization to search someone's property), the detectives working the case visit the suspects, and possible evidence is sealed— including a loaded pistol from each suspect. Below is what the **forensics lab** discovers when comparing the evidence from the bank with the evidence the detectives have seized. Study it carefully. When you're done, see if you can solve the crime!

1. Jacket fibers from each suspect's jacket.

Richard Mantellino

Jack Leetch

Kieran O'Sullivan

2. A hair sample obtained from each suspect.

Richard Mantellino

Jack Leetch

Kieran O'Sullivan

3. A fired bullet obtained by ballistics techs after test-firing each suspect's gun.

Richard Mantellino

Jack Leetch

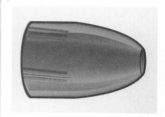

Kieran O'Sullivan

4. Medical records, indicating each suspect's age, health, and blood type.

HEALTH INSURANCE FORM DATE CMD

PATIENT'S NAME (Last, First, MI) | D.O.B. | AGE | SEX
Richard Mantellino | 10/31/1974 | 30 | M
PATIENT'S ADDRESS:
147 Roebling
BLOOD TYPE
O
NOTES:

Richard Mantellino

HOSPITAL ADMITTANCE FORM

PATIENT'S NAME (Last, First, MI) | D.O.B. | AGE | SEX
Jack Leetch | 4/18/1976 | 28 | M
PATIENT'S ADDRESS:
555 Broadway
BLOOD TYPE
O
NOTES:

Jack Leetch

HEALTH INSURANCE FORM

PATIENT'S NAME (Last, First, MI) | D.O.B. | AGE | SEX
Kieran O'Sullivan | 5/4/1975 | 27 | M
PATIENT'S ADDRESS:
1660 Pennsylvania Ave.
BLOOD TYPE
A
NOTES:
Suffers from asthma

Kieran O'Sullivan

5. A handwriting sample from each suspect.

Phone List

Mom   555-3456
Dad's work 555-7822

Richard Mantellino

Grocery List
-eggs
-milk
-coffee

Jack Leetch

Things to do:
-clean bathroom
- Go shopping
- Pay Bills

Kieran O'Sullivan

After comparing the above **forensic analysis** with the **crime scene** evidence, who are you going to **collar**?

CASE CLOSED

Case File #1: Funny Money pages 10–11

Part II.

1. Look on the back of the bill on the right and left sides. You should see a bunch of tiny 20s in gold print.

2. On the front of the bill on the trim, "The United States of America 20 USA 20 USA" is printed.

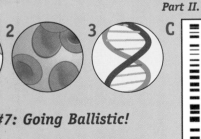

Case File #5: Try Not to Faint! pages 19–21,

Part II. As you learned in this activity, rookie, blood spatters differently depending on the height from which it falls, and the force with which it's spread. So if there are just a few drops at the scene—chances are great that the person involved isn't bleeding a lot. That could mean the person is only slightly cut—or that their injuries weren't made by anything sharp.

As you also saw, "flicked" blood has a certain long, spraying splatter pattern, due to the force it's traveling at. If this sort of splatter is at a crime scene, chances are there was a pretty serious wound to someone—and that a struggle of some sort probably occurred. A flicked pattern is not going to occur for someone with just a slight bloody nose, that's for sure!

Case File #6: DNA—An Investigator's Best Friend pages 22–24

Part I.   **Part II.**

1   2   3   C

Case File #7: Going Ballistic! pages 26–28

2. **A**

3. **C**

Case File #8: Know Your Writes pages 30–32

Part I. The sentence, "The quick brown fox jumped over the lazy dogs" has every letter of the alphabet in it at least once! That's why the sentence is often used to check someone's handwriting. Every possible letter a person could write is represented.

Case File #9: An Ace in the Hole pages 34–35

The clerk states that he only heard one shot, but you have two bullet holes—the two shots must have gone off at the same time! And that means that both perps fired. Since the angle of entry for each shot shows that the shots were "straight on," without any left or right angle—the shots had to come from right in front of the clerk. So there was no third perp!

If you examined the angles of entry carefully, rookie, you should have noted that bullet hole #1 shows an upward angle of entry. Since we know that Perp A pointed his gun at the clerk as the clerk ducked down—that means his shot would have a downward angle of entry. So Perp A's bullet hole couldn't be #1. Perp B must be responsible for #1! If you examine bullet hole #2, you'll see it shows a downward angle of entry—just like the one you saw pictured on page 34. And that means Perp A is responsible for bullet hole #2!

Case of the Armed Robbery pages 45–47

1. The fiber from Jack Leetch's jacket matches best.
2. Both Richard Mantellino and Jack Leetch are a pretty close match to the hair found at the crime scene. Kieran O'Sullivan's hair is just a bit too curly.
3. Jack Leetch's bullet matches the one found at the crime scene.
4. Both Richard Mantellino and Jack Leetch match the type found at the crime scene—type O.
5. Jack Leetch's handwriting is the closest to the ransom note. Kieran O'Sullivan's has some similarities, and Richard Mantellino's handwriting isn't at all similar.

So rookie: Who is the common denominator in all the above evidence? Only **Jack Leetch** matches across the board with *all* aspects of the evidence. Plus: Kieran O'Sullivan has the wrong blood type—so he *can't* be the perp. And Richard Mantellino's handwriting isn't even close. Put that together with the direct match between the rifling in Jack Leetch's gun and the bullet found at the crime scene, and you've got your man!